Felicia Cartright

and the
Lonely Teacher

Felicia

Joan

FELICIA CARTRIGHT

AND THE
LONELY TEACHER

BERNARD PALMER

Felicia Cartright and the Lonely Teacher
© 2025 by Bernard Palmer
All rights reserved. First edition 1960.
Second edition 2025.

Scripture quotations from The Authorized (King James)
Version. Rights in the Authorized Version in the United
Kingdom are vested in the Crown. Reproduced by permission
of the Crown's patentee, Cambridge University Press.

Cover Artwork: Ideogram
Editor: Charlene Miskimen

Aneko Press Youth

www.anekopress.com

Aneko Press, Life Sentence Publishing, and our logos are trademarks of
Life Sentence Publishing, Inc.
203 E. Birch Street
P.O. Box 652
Abbotsford, WI 54405

JUVENILE FICTION / Religious / Christian / Action & Adventure

Paperback ISBN: 979-8-88936-296-8

eBook ISBN: 979-8-88936-297-5

10   9   8   7   6   5   4   3   2   1

Available where books are sold

CONTENTS

CHAPTER 1

THE CLOSED DOOR

It was late afternoon at Wellington School for Girls. The day had been bleak and chilly. Like so many fall days in New England, it was ugly and gray, wearing the wind in its hair and frost in its teeth. It withered the last remnants of Miss Duncan's beloved garden outside the Administration Building and started to paint the leaves of the gigantic oaks and maples with delicate, iridescent colors.

The sun came out briefly, about noon, to whisper seductively of the summer just past. It brought students out of their sweaters and caused them to languish on the walks between classes. But the respite was short.

Clouds closed in, and temperatures dropped again.

Felicia Cartright buttoned her coat and hurried up the steps of the gray, ivy-covered dorm. She was slight and diminutive, with a delicate turned-up nose and dancing blue eyes. She was always busy. In fact, she gave the appearance of breathless activity, even as she stopped inside the lounge.

"Hi, Felicia," somebody called from across the lounge. "Did you get them?"

She took the scarf from her neck and rubbed her hands.

"Miss Duncan forgot to pick the roses last night," she said. "They were all frozen, and so am I."

"Worse luck," Wendy Adams said. "About the roses, I mean."

"So you don't care what happens to me," Felicia countered good-naturedly.

"Everybody cares what happens to you, Felicia," Wendy went on. "It's just that a bouquet of roses would have been beautiful on the center table at the banquet tomorrow night."

Felicia went up to the room she shared with Joan Bailey.

Joan was sitting at the desk chewing on a stub of a pencil.

"Hi," she said without looking up. "How's mother's little helper?"

"Not much help. I'm afraid," Felicia answered. She hung her coat on a hanger and went over to the radiator. "Miss Duncan forgot to pick the roses last night. They all froze."

Joan shuddered. "What a blast of cold air there'll be in the office for a few days," she said. "I hope I'm able to avoid it."

"You won't if you don't get that English theme finished by tomorrow," Felicia told her.

"Oh, that!" her friend answered carelessly. "Didn't I tell you? I'm getting an extension of time."

"Wonderful," Felicia replied. "Does Miss Merton know it yet?"

"That's why I've been waiting for you," the dark-haired girl said. "We're going down to see her this afternoon."

Felicia pulled out a chair and sat down.

"Honestly, Joan," she said with the frankness and exasperation permitted by long years of close friendship, "you've had plenty of time to finish your theme. I wouldn't blame Miss Duncan if she'd flunk you out of Wellington. I wouldn't blame her at all."

"Oh, I'm not worried about that!" Joan said. "She needs me here. She has to have someone as the horrible example. She can say to new students, 'Now you'd better study. You don't want to be like Joan Bailey, do you?'"

Felicia laughed and shook her head.

"I don't know why I worry about your grades," she said. "You certainly don't."

"You just don't know," Joan countered. "I've been worried terribly about this English theme. It's supposed to count for half our grade."

"You've been worried *terribly*," Felicia went on, "for about fifteen minutes."

Joan got to her feet.

"But you will go with me to see Miss Merton, won't you?" she asked. "I'll do all the talking. I just want you along for moral support."

"I'll go," Felicia said, "but I'm warning you. I'm on Miss Merton's side. She's new here. She's not on to you yet."

Her roommate gasped.

"Felicia Cartright!" she exclaimed. "I'm cut to the heart! After the way you and I have bled and died together! To think that you would desert me!"

"Come on," Felicia said, "before you drown in your tears."

"If I don't get that extension, Miss Duncan will skin me. She'll skin me alive."

"If you'd thought of that a week ago," Felicia reminded her, "you wouldn't be in this mess."

"But the themes weren't due a week ago," Joan answered.

They left the dormitory and went across the cold, wind-swept campus to the English instructor's room.

Felicia shivered as the raw wind tore at them. "Sometimes I wonder why I didn't choose a school in southern California or Florida."

Joan laughed.

"Now, Felicia," she said, "you know you wouldn't be happy anywhere else but at dear old Wellington. Even the climate is part of the training. Wellington girls are taught to face life; to meet every situation."

"Except," her companion added, "getting English themes in on time."

"I'm going to work on that theme tonight," Joan said. "I'm going to get this extension because I can't possibly finish a research theme for tomorrow's class. Then I'm going to start work right after dinner and stay at it every night until I finish."

In spite of herself, Felicia laughed. She, and the rest of the class, had been at work for a couple of weeks on the research theme.

They paused momentarily before the door to Miss Merton's room.

Joan knocked lightly.

There was no response.

"I don't believe there's anyone in there," Felicia said. "I don't hear anyone."

Joan rapped on the door again.

"Maybe she's already gone for the night," Felicia went on.

"That couldn't be. It isn't five o'clock. And you know what the manual says: In the Wellington tradition, teachers are available for consultation with students in their rooms until five o'clock each school day.'"

"Just the same," Felicia said, "she doesn't answer."

Joan turned the doorknob quietly and opened the door.

"Oh!" she gasped under her breath.

Miss Merton was sitting at her desk, her head

buried in her arms and her shoulders twitching convulsively. A sob escaped her lips.

The girls stared at one another in bewilderment. Joan would have turned back and closed the door, but not Felicia. She approached the desk quietly.

"Miss Merton," she said, her voice soft and tender, "is there something wrong?"

At the sound of her voice, the young teacher looked up. Her lips trembled, and her face was white. A lone tear trickled, unheeded, down her cheek.

"What are you doing in here?" she demanded. "Don't you know you are supposed to knock?"

"We did knock," Joan managed, "but you didn't answer, so we–"

"So you came bursting in," Miss Merton continued. "From now on, when my door is closed, you are to wait until I open it. Is that clear?"

"I–I'm sorry," Felicia apologized.

"Now, if you'll excuse me, I have a frightful headache."

She turned deliberately away from them.

Felicia and Joan fled.

"What do you suppose brought that on?" Joan asked.

"She's terribly upset about something," the other girl answered. There was a short silence. "What do you suppose it is?"

"Now don't start that," Joan cautioned. "We have enough trouble of our own."

"But she isn't the sort to cry that way," Felicia went on. "And she isn't the kind of person to get so furious at us over a little thing like going into her room before she told us to. She must be in trouble, Joan. Real trouble."

"She's not alone," Joan said. "You remember I've got an English theme due tomorrow, and I haven't even written it."

"We were there. Why didn't you ask her?"

"Are you kidding? We were having enough trouble without asking for any more."

They started back to their room.

"I can't get Miss Merton out of my mind," Felicia said. "Did you see that letter on her desk? I think that must have been what she was crying about."

"It was probably from a boyfriend," Joan answered.

"You sound very sure of yourself."

"It's got to be," her roommate continued. "We've seen a lot of girls here at Wellington crying over letters. But you never saw anyone crying over a letter from her parents or her brothers or sisters or even a friend. Nope, when the tears start to flow, it's always because of a boy."

"When did you take up psychology, *Doctor* Bailey?" Felicia laughed.

"That's not psychology. That's just plain, old common sense."

"I suppose I can get a start on that English theme tonight," Joan said as they walked down the corridor after dinner. "But it's really a waste of time. I can't possibly finish it."

"Now you're trying to talk yourself out of getting to work."

They opened the door and stopped short.

"Miss Merton!" Felicia gasped. "What are you doing here?"

The instructor was sitting at Felicia's desk. Make up did a fair job of hiding the ravages of the tears, but her eyes were sad, and her face was haggard. Ordinarily she was very attractive, but that night she looked very tired and at least half again as old as her twenty-five years.

"I took the liberty of doing the same thing I became so angry at you for doing," she said. "I came in and sat down. But I had to talk with you tonight."

Joan closed the door.

"Is there something we can do for you?" she asked.

"This isn't easy for a teacher," Miss Merton said, "but will you please forgive me for losing my temper? There was no call to fly off that way."

"We're the ones who owe the apology," Felicia told her. "We had no right to open your door when you had it closed."

Miss Merton was fighting to control her emotions.

"I have been faced with some personal problems lately," she said, "that have been almost overwhelming. I was embarrassed to have you see me crying. That's why I lost my temper."

Felicia and Joan both smiled.

"You can be sure," Joan said, "that we're not going to say anything about this."

"Thank you, girls," Miss Merton answered. "You cannot know how much I appreciate that. However, it is not the reason I came."

Felicia nodded.

There was a short, painful silence.

"There was some reason you girls came to see me," Miss Merton said, "and I rudely sent you away."

"I wanted to talk with you about the English theme that's due tomorrow," Joan said, "but I dislike doing it now. You may think I'm trying to take advantage of a situation."

Miss Merton smiled.

"Your theme is supposed to be finished by class time tomorrow," the teacher said, "and yours isn't quite ready. Is that it?"

"How did you know?" Joan blurted. "Has Felicia been talking to you?"

"Not at all. Your reputation has gone before you. As a matter of fact, Miss Duncan told me you occasionally experience difficulty in meeting deadlines."

Joan managed a sick, little grin.

"I suppose it's all off then," she said. "I guess I'll learn."

"I have already decided I was a little too severe in expecting the themes to be finished by tomorrow," the teacher said. "So I am going to give everyone until the first of the week to finish. Will that help?"

"I think I can have it by that time," Joan said. "At least I ought to have most of it finished."

"I'm sure you can." Miss Merton got to her feet and looked directly at Joan. "I do hope you can have it in on time. I shouldn't like to be forced to take five percent off your grade for each day it's late."

Joan recoiled at the stiff penalty.

"I want you both to know I am sorry that I talked the way I did a little while ago," the teacher said. And with that she was gone.

"Did you see that look on her face?" Felicia asked. "Did you ever see anyone look so concerned and bewildered?"

Joan crossed to the bed and sat down.

"And to think," she said, "Miss Merton came all the way over here to apologize to us. It makes me ashamed of all the nasty things I was thinking about her."

Felicia went to the window and looked out. In the semidarkness of early evening, she could make out the figure of their teacher as she walked down the steps and across the campus toward the private home where she had a room. Her shoulders sagged, and she seemed to move only with concerted effort.

"What do you suppose is troubling her?" Felicia asked.

CHAPTER 2

THE ANSWER

During the next few days, Joan worked steadily on her research theme. She checked out books from the library and read them during lunch hour, and between bites she scribbled her notes.

"Look who's getting so studious all of a sudden," one of the girls said laughing. "What happened, Joan? Did you suddenly decide you want to be valedictorian? Or is it a scholarship you're bucking for?"

Joan turned to her.

"Did you ever see a picture of a guy paddling like everything to keep from being swept over a falls like Niagara? Well, that's me. I'm at the place where I've got to run as fast as I can just to stay in the same place."

"Don't tell me. Let me guess. It's Miss Merton's English class, and you're working on your research theme."

"You've been peeking," Joan told her.

The group at the table rocked with laughter.

While Joan was battling to finish her theme before the deadline, Felicia was doing a little quiet research of her own. She visited with the registrar, the head of the English Department, and even gleaned a little information about Miss Merton from Miss Duncan.

"Of course, I wasn't able to come right out and ask them a lot of questions," she confided to her room-mate a few nights later. "But I am beginning to find out some things."

"So am I," Joan answered. "Namely, that it is much better to get an English theme finished in plenty of time than to wait until just before the axe comes down."

"I learned that she is from New Hampshire," Felicia said, keeping her voice low. "She is twenty-five years old. She graduated from the university with a master's degree last spring. Her parents are both dead, and, apparently, she has no living relatives. That could account for her loneliness."

"How about boyfriends?" Joan asked. "It's a boy-friend causing all the trouble."

"A boyfriend?" Felicia echoed, her voice scornful. "Is that all you can think of, Joan?"

"You want to help her, don't you? Then find the boyfriend, patch up the quarrel, and everything will be hunky dory. I'm telling you, it's as simple as that."

"I don't think so," Felicia answered after a time.

"Do you realize we never see her with any of the other teachers, and we seldom see her smile or laugh?"

Joan pushed aside her theme.

"I know she's upset about something," she acknowledged, "but there's nothing we can do about it except to pray for her."

"I wonder," the other girl replied. "She seemed so eager to talk with us the other night when she came to apologize. I think we might help just by being friendly."

"Like what?" Joan asked.

"Taking her out to dinner tomorrow night."

Joan's forehead wrinkled.

"I'm always interested in anything where there's eating involved," she said. "It sounds great."

"Then let's go and ask her right now," Felicia said.

"It sounds great, except that there's a little thing called money."

"Don't tell me you're broke again!" Felicia exclaimed.

"Flatter than flat," Joan answered. "You see, last month I borrowed on this month's allowance. And this month I borrowed on next month's allowance, and now Dad says I've got to get on a cash basis. No more money until I'm squared away." She sighed wearily. "So I'm practically a pauper for the next thirty days."

"All right," Felicia said. "I'll finance the dinner."

Joan smiled. "Now that is what I call a friend. A true, dyed-in-the-wool friend. Honestly, Felicia,

I didn't know what a jewel I was getting when you and I started to room together."

"That sweet talk is going to get you nowhere. I am still taking an IOU for your share of the dinner."

Joan shrugged her shoulders in exaggerated resignation.

"Shylock!" she said. "The trouble with you is that you've been around Miss Duncan too long. You've lost your faith in human nature."

"The trouble with me," Felicia said laughing, "is that I've been around you long enough to learn all about you. I just don't fool so easily anymore."

"Oh, well," Joan answered, "such is life! If you want to make me miserable hounding me about an IOU, I suppose that's your privilege."

They went down to Miss Duncan's office, signed out to see Miss Merton, and left the campus.

The wind was blowing along the deserted street, rattling the leaves in the trees above them.

"Do you suppose she'll go with us?" Joan asked. "Some teachers are not too keen on running around with students."

"We don't want to run around with her," Felicia said. "We just want to be friendly."

They crossed the street and headed for the house where Miss Merton lived.

"Wow!" Joan exclaimed. "Look at that snazzy car!"

There was a brilliant, red sports car at the curb. Joan turned to Felicia triumphantly.

"Now what did I tell you about a boyfriend?" she demanded. "They had a little argument and Miss Merton got all upset about it. Now he's here to make up, and everything will be all right again. She'll come to class in the morning as chipper as a love bird."

"We don't even know that the owner of this car is calling on Miss Merton. There are several teachers staying here, you know."

"And I can tell you this much," Joan said, "I don't intend to go up and find out. If we burst in on her now and she's entertaining her boyfriend, I'd sure get a failing grade on that research theme."

"I suppose you're right, but I'm going to make sure he's here to see Miss Merton and not someone else before we leave."

They moved along the hedge toward the walk that led to the front steps. As they neared the gate, Felicia saw the bright glow of a cigarette on the porch and the dark figure of a man.

"Wade," they heard Miss Merton say in desperation, "why did you follow me here? Why did you have to find out where I am?"

Felicia and Joan stood still.

"You know you can't run away from me, Cindy!" a man's voice retorted. "We're engaged! Doesn't that mean anything to you?"

The silence was deafening.

"Doesn't it?" he demanded.

"I returned your ring, Wade," she said. "That should be answer enough."

"But it's not," he countered, "I want an explanation, Cindy, and I'm going to stay right here until I get it."

Felicia turned to Joan and whispered, "Come on, we shouldn't stand here eavesdropping."

"I tried to explain to you," Miss Merton continued. "You got my letter, didn't you?"

"I don't call *that* an explanation!"

"Well," Joan said when they were out of hearing distance, "we're not going to worry about Miss Merton anymore. He'll talk her into making up, and that will be that."

"I hope not," Felicia said.

"What makes you say that?"

"I'm not sure. I didn't like it that he smokes, but I think it's something more than that. He sounded so belligerent and so-so worldly or something. He just doesn't seem to be Miss Merton's type."

"Maybe not," Joan said. "But they'll make up. You can count on that."

CHAPTER 3

BACK AGAIN!

The following morning when Felicia and Joan entered their English class, Miss Merton was sitting at her desk. Her face was sallow and pinched, and her eyes were dull.

"Good morning," Felicia said brightly.

But it was as though the teacher had not heard. She was shuffling through a stack of papers with trembling fingers.

Joan caught her roommate's eye and nodded significantly.

Several times during class that morning Miss Merton would start to say something, then stop as though her mind wandered to something else.

"Miss Merton," one of the girls said toward the end of the period, "are you going to collect our English themes today? You told us last week we'd have to have them ready by this morning."

"Your English themes?" the instructor repeated. "Oh! Oh, yes. I'll collect them this morning. Thank you for reminding me."

When the class was over, Felicia took Joan by the arm and went to the teacher's desk.

"Miss Merton," she began.

The teacher looked up. "Yes, Felicia," she said.

"Joan and I are going out to dinner tonight," she said. "We'd like to have you go with us."

For a minute Miss Merton did not reply. "I'm sorry," she began. "There's something else I must do."

"Perhaps another time," Joan said.

They turned to go to their next class. Miss Merton got up quickly and stopped them.

"I–I'm so sorry I was rude just now," she said. "I think I can postpone what I have planned. That is, if you would like me to have dinner with you."

"We'll meet you in the dorm lounge at six," Felicia answered.

Miss Merton smiled gratefully.

"Thank you," she said. "I know I'll enjoy it very much." She paused. "This is the first time I've been invited out since I came to Wellington."

"I can't figure her out," Joan said when they were out on the campus. "I thought everything was all right, and now she acts as though she's more despondent than ever."

Felicia nodded.

"But she was glad for our invitation to dinner."

A few minutes before six, the girls went down to the lounge. Miss Merton was already there. She wore a lovely, yellow dress that seemed to deepen the color of her eyes. She was almost happy.

"I was feeling terribly low this morning," she said as they left the dorm, "when you girls asked me out to dinner. You'll never know how much your invitation picked me up."

They took Joan's car and drove to a little cafe a mile or so from Wellington. The girls ate there frequently, and the waiter knew them.

"Good evening," he said smiling. "And how are things over at the school these days?"

"As hard as ever, Henri," Joan said. "The trouble is they all pick on me."

"*Oui,*" he answered, the grin still on his face. "Maybe they are determined to give you the education, no?"

"I'm afraid you're right. And I've got to admit it's not easy. Do you have a table for us?"

"Your same little table?" he asked, starting across the floor ahead of them. "Over here by the window?"

"What a lovely place," Miss Merton observed.

"You wait one moment," Henri told them, "and I put on the favorite music for you, no?"

"You seem to be favored customers," Miss Merton said.

"Henri is a jewel," Felicia said. "I think he makes a hobby of trying to do nice things for people."

"You know," Henri said to Felicia as he came to take their orders, "I read the book of John."

"That's fine," she answered. "What did you think of it?"

"Beautiful. Beautiful. But there are so many things I not understand." Henri sighed deeply. "I am like that Nicodemus, I guess. I keep asking myself how a man can be born a second time when he is old."

"Our first birth is physical. And being born physically is the only way we can get into this world."

"Oui," he acknowledged.

"Our second birth is spiritual," Felicia went on. "The only way we can be saved and have eternal life in heaven is by being born spiritually into the heavenly kingdom. We do that by recognizing that we are lost sinners and by placing our trust in Jesus Christ for salvation."

A perplexed look crossed Henri's face.

"One time when we are not so busy," he said, "I sit down with you, and we talk. There are so many questions."

When he was gone, Miss Merton turned to Felicia.

"You must be a Christian," she said.

"I am," the girl answered. "We both have put our trust in Christ. We talk with Henri about Christian things almost every time we come in. He is interested and all that and acts as though he wants to know more, but he will go only so far. There's something holding him back."

"Felicia is the one who led me to Christ," Joan said. "Before I became a Christian, I was so self-centered and headstrong, I didn't think of anyone or anything except myself." She paused. "I guess I'm not much different now as far as I personally am concerned. It's just that Christ has helped me to be a little more considerate of others."

"I think it is good," Miss Merton said, "that you witness that way."

"We've learned," Felicia continued, "to trust God for everything. He has the answer for all our problems. And not just the little ones. He has the answers to our big problems too, those that are so big we don't know which way to turn."

Henri came with their food. They bowed their heads, and Joan asked the blessing in low tones, but clearly audible. When she finished, Miss Merton looked up.

"A moment ago, Felicia," the teacher said suddenly, "you said God has the answer to all our problems."

The girl nodded. "We've always found it so."

"And so have I," Miss Merton went on. "But I'm afraid I've had trouble remembering it these past days. You see, I'm a Christian too."

"How wonderful!" Joan exclaimed.

The teacher hesitated briefly.

"I wonder if you would join me in prayer about something?" she asked.

"Of course, we will," Felicia answered.

"I told you the other day that I have a problem that is almost overwhelming," she continued. "Certain Christian people have advised me strongly against doing what I've been considering. I've tried to follow their advice, but I'm not sure now. I want to do it very, very much."

"I see," Felicia replied. "And how do you want us to pray?"

Miss Merton looked up quickly.

"I–I–" she began, "I don't know."

They finished eating in comparative silence.

"That was a lovely meal," Miss Merton said as they left the cafe. "I don't know when I have enjoyed an evening so much."

They were waiting for the traffic light to change when a red sports car came around the corner and stopped at the curb beside them.

"Cindy!" the driver called to her.

Felicia and Joan recognized the voice.

"Wade Loring!" Miss Merton exclaimed. "I thought you were back home!"

"I was," he retorted, "but I came back. And I'm coming back until I get this mess straightened out." He leaned over and opened the door. "Come on. I want to talk to you."

"But, Wade," she protested, "I can't go with you now. I'm with Felicia and Joan."

She introduced them to him. He acknowledged the introduction.

"Now, are you coming with me or not?" he demanded. "If you don't, it's all off! You and I are through!"

"Will you girls excuse me?" Miss Merton asked. "Wade has driven a long way to see me."

"Certainly," Felicia said. "We've got to get back to the dorm before 'lights out' anyway."

"And thank you very much," Miss Merton said, "for a lovely evening."

"Come on," Wade Loring said gruffly. "I've already spent an hour and a half looking for you."

She got into the car, and he went roaring away.

CHAPTER 4

AN UNEXPECTED CALLER

During class the rest of the week, Miss Merton seemed to avoid Felicia and Joan. She spoke cordially enough and was friendly in and out of class, but she gave them no opportunity to be alone with her. So it was something of a surprise when she invited them to spend Saturday with her.

"I'm going to the afternoon symphony concert, and I would like to have you join me. We'll come back to the house afterward for pizza."

"That sounds exciting!" Felicia exclaimed.

"And," Miss Merton went on, "I won't leave you in the lurch as I did the other night. I promise."

"That was all right," Joan told her. "We understood."

They went to Boston in Miss Merton's car and attended the concert. The teacher was apparently having a good time, but she talked little and seldom laughed.

"It will be a little late when we eat," she said as they left the auditorium. "Why don't we stop for a milkshake before driving home?"

"A great idea," Joan said.

In the booth, Miss Merton leaned forward intently.

"I owe you an apology for leaving you the way I did," she said.

"We've already forgotten it," Joan assured her.

"But I haven't. It was terribly rude."

The waiter brought their shakes.

"I know you won't say anything about what I'm going to tell you," the young woman went on.

"You can depend on us."

"When I was in high school," she began, "I didn't have dates like other girls. I tried to pretend that it didn't make any difference, but it did. It hurt terribly."

Felicia and Joan glanced at one another. It was a little embarrassing to have Miss Merton talk that way, and yet they felt she wanted to continue.

"I used to be afraid I was one of those girls who would never have a chance to marry," she continued. "And like most girls, I wanted a home and a family of my own more than anything else in the world." She breathed deeply. "In fact, I still do."

"I know how you feel," Felicia said.

Miss Merton laughed nervously.

"I don't know why I'm telling you these things," she said, "but I've got to tell you."

It was a moment before she could talk again.

"Then when I was in my last year of college, Wade Loring came along. I don't know yet how he ever came to be interested in me. He could have had half the girls at the university if he'd wanted them."

Miss Merton's voice was steady, but her lips quivered, and now and then she stopped.

"It has bothered me a great deal that he isn't a Christian," she said. "Sometimes I think it might be possible for me to lead him to Christ after we're married. Then again, I've been sure it would never work out. In fact, after Mom died, I determined to break up with him."

"But he hunted until he found you teaching school here at Wellington," Joan said. "Is that it?"

"Exactly. It would have been so simple if I'd never started going with him. But now I think so much of him that–that I don't know for sure what I want to do. I want to follow God's will for my life, but I don't see how I can give up Wade."

"We'll surely pray for you," Joan said.

Miss Merton smiled.

"Thank you," she said. "You know, I had a difficult time deciding whether I should burden you with all this or not, but I'm glad I did. Just talking with you and knowing that you'll pray is a big help."

They finished their shakes and went out to the car. Miss Merton drove expertly through the traffic to her apartment.

"Now," she said, "to whip up that pizza. I'm starved."

As they opened the door to the stairs, her land-lady, Mrs. Johnson, called to her.

"There you are, Miss Merton," she said. "You've had company this afternoon. A gentleman."

Miss Merton blanched.

"Was it Mr. Loring?" she asked. "The man who has been here to see me a couple of times during the past week?"

Mrs. Johnson shook her head.

"No," she replied, "this is a much older man. He talked as though he must see you on some very urgent business. He asked me to tell you he had been here and that he will come back about seven."

"Thank you," Miss Merton answered. "We're eating here this evening."

"Perhaps Joan and I had better leave," Felicia suggested. "If you have business to discuss, we can come back another time."

"No," the instructor said quickly, "I want you to stay. There is nothing anyone could want to see me about that is secret."

As they were clearing the table, there was a knock on the door and Miss Merton went to open it.

"Why, Mr. Gardell!" she exclaimed. "What are you doing here?"

"How are you, Cindy?"

He was a tall, portly individual with gray hair and a kindly, sympathetic face.

She introduced him to the girls and asked him to sit down.

"Had a terrible time finding you, Cindy," he said reproachfully. "You left no forwarding address."

She nodded without explaining.

He glanced at Joan and Felicia.

"Would it be possible for me to speak to you privately?" he asked.

"That's not necessary, Mr. Gardell. I'm sure we can trust Felicia and Joan to be discreet about anything they might hear."

"We should be going anyway," Joan said quickly. She got to her feet, but Miss Merton stopped her.

"Please!" she said. "I want you to stay."

Reluctantly Joan returned to her chair.

"I suppose you're right, Cindy," Mr. Gardell said. "There really is nothing to be secretive about."

He opened his briefcase.

"You know, of course," he continued, "that I have been your family's lawyer for years and am handling your mother's estate."

"Yes," Miss Merton said. "I thought probably this had something to do with that. Do you have papers you want me to sign?"

"Not at the moment. We're still negotiating the sale of the house."

"I see."

"The thing that brought me here is of a rather personal nature."

He found the folder he was looking for.

"You have been aware of the fact that you were adopted, were you not?"

She nodded.

"Mom and Dad didn't try to hide it from me."

"Did your mother ever tell you anything about your birth parents?" he asked. "Who they were? Where they lived? How they happened to place you out for adoption?"

"She told me I came from a good family," Miss Merton said quietly, "that my father died, and mother married again. But names and places didn't seem very important."

"And I would have agreed with you," Mr. Gardell said, "until we went through your mother's papers and came across this."

He handed her a folded sheet of paper.

"Why, it's in Mom's handwriting!" she exclaimed.

"'Dear Cindy' she read aloud. "'Dad and I decided a long while ago not to tell you this, but as the end draws near, I cannot keep it any longer. The little tin box–'"

"What does it mean?" Miss Merton asked.

He shook his head. "I have no idea, Cindy."

"But is this all of it?" she asked. "Isn't there another sheet?"

"We've been through everything," he told her. "Whether your mother decided not to write any more or got tired writing since she was very weak near the last and then didn't finish before she passed away, I don't know."

Miss Merton read the note once more and folded it.

"It may mean nothing," Mr. Gardell said. "And then again–"

He got to his feet.

"I remember your dad telling me once that they had gotten you from a wealthy family. It may be that you are entitled to a share in some large estate."

Miss Merton was not even listening.

"I remember that little tin box," she said. "Mom and Dad always kept it locked. As a little girl, I used to pretend I was a fairy queen, and I kept my crown and my jewels and my magic scepter in it."

She smiled.

"The only spanking I remember Dad giving me was when I got the key and started to open the box. I never tried it again, but I always wondered what was in it. It was the one big mystery in my life."

"It ought to be a simple matter to find out what this is all about," Joan said. "Just get the box and open it."

"I'm afraid it's not quite as simple as that," the lawyer said. "We have searched the house and garage thoroughly. The tin box is gone!"

CHAPTER 5

NEWSPAPER HEADLINE!

Miss Merton went down to the door with Mr. Gardell, and they talked in low tones.

"What do you make of that?" Felicia asked Joan in an excited whisper.

Joan shook her head.

"I don't think I've ever heard anything so strange," she said. "Just imagine what that's like. Miss Merton doesn't know who her birth parents are, and she may never know unless they can find that little tin box."

The teacher returned soon. There was a tired smile on her face.

"My life isn't always like this, I assure you."

Felicia and Joan stared at one another and at Miss Merton. For a long while no one spoke.

"I know this is none of our affair," Felicia said at last. "But are you going to try to find the tin box? Is there anything we can do to help you?"

"I don't see how I can possibly locate it if Mr. Gardell and his associates couldn't find it. He's one of the best lawyers in our county, and I know he would put good men on the case until the box was found or he was sure it wasn't anywhere around."

Her face grew thoughtful. "Still, I would like to know what's in it."

"It may be you're rich and don't know it," Joan said.

"I don't think that's very likely," Miss Merton went on. "At least I'm not concerned about it. The thing I'm most interested in is learning who I really am. Just think, I may have brothers and sisters somewhere! I've always wondered about that. And Mother may even still be living. If she is, I–I'd like to see her. That's the thing that interests me."

"Do you suppose it would do any good to look for the box yourself?" Felicia suggested. "Joan and I would be glad to go with you if you'd like to have us."

"I'll say we would," Joan put in. "I'm so excited already, I can scarcely stand it."

The teacher's eyes brightened.

"Would you go with me?" she asked. "That would be wonderful. I wouldn't like to go back to the house and rummage through things alone."

They made plans to go to Miss Merton's hometown the following weekend.

"And," the teacher said, as the girls finally headed back to the dormitory, "we want to be careful not to say anything about this to anyone. People are certain to put the wrong interpretation on it, and it might be that publicity could actually keep us from finding out what we want to know."

Felicia and Joan both nodded in agreement.

The following morning, the girls went to Sunday school and church as usual. When services were over, they returned to the school for dinner.

"I'm starved," Joan said.

"You're always starved," Felicia told her.

The lounge was crowded, but they found a place on a small couch across the room. Felicia had just picked up a magazine when Miss Merton came in. Her face was flushed, and there was a peculiar look in her eyes. She ran up the steps and stopped, looking quickly around. She carried a newspaper in her hand.

Joan spotted her almost immediately. "There's Miss Merton," she said. "I think she's looking for us."

The teacher saw her and came hurrying across the lounge.

"Is there something wrong?" Joan asked.

"I'm afraid there's something terribly wrong," Miss Merton said in guarded tones. "May we go up to your room for a moment?"

They left the crowded lounge, aware that practically everyone was watching them. When they entered their room, Miss Merton opened the day's paper.

"Mrs. Johnson just showed me this," she said.

Felicia and Joan both stared at the front-page item.

"'WELLINGTON INSTRUCTOR IN MYSTERY

ROLE,'" she quoted the headlines. "'Miss Cynthia Merton, new English instructor at exclusive Wellington School for Girls, is the center of a knotty mystery this morning. . . .

"'Adopted by the late Mr. and Mrs. Henry Merton more than twenty years ago, her identity, if known, has never been disclosed. On Wednesday of this week, a strange, unfinished note in the late Mrs. Merton's handwriting was found. . . .'"

The account went on to reveal the contents of the note and to say that the little tin box could not be found.

"'Clay Gardell, New Hampshire attorney handling the modest Merton estate, refused to comment,'" it concluded, "'beyond the guess that Miss Merton might actually be the member of some wealthy, socially prominent family.'"

"How did the papers get the story?" Felicia asked.

Miss Merton shook her head.

"I certainly didn't give it to them," she said. "And I know you girls didn't."

"The reporter talked with Mr. Gardell," Joan said. "They even quote him." She grasped Miss Merton by the arm. "Do you suppose he could have given out the account?"

"I don't see why he would do that," Miss Merton said. "He didn't even want to talk in front of you."

"You know how interested Mrs. Johnson was," Felicia said. "Do you suppose she could have eaves-dropped last night and given the story to a reporter?"

"Possibly," the teacher said. "But whoever did it or whatever happened to tip off the papers, it happened shortly after Mr. Gardell came to see me, or it would never have made this morning's paper."

"That's right," Felicia said.

"What effect do you think this will have on our finding the tin box and unscrambling the riddle of the note?" Joan asked.

"It's not going to help any," the teacher said. "That's for sure. It would have been bad enough if the story had been local. But it was picked up by the wire services and published all across the country."

"Do you think that will have any effect on our finding the box?" Felicia asked.

"It could if it brings out curiosity seekers to look for it. I wish it hadn't happened, but there's no use in worrying about it now."

Felicia sighed deeply.

"I don't see why it had to happen," she said.

"I just came over to tell you," Miss Merton went on, "that if reporters should try to pump you, don't give them any more information than you have to. The quicker this story dies out the better it will be."

"They won't get any information from me," Joan said. "I don't know anything. And that's the truth. Ask anybody."

Miss Merton smiled.

"I wouldn't say you don't know anything, Joan. Let's just say that you'll go to considerable lengths to keep others from finding out whether you know anything or not."

CHAPTER 6

THE MYSTERY DEEPENS

Reporters did not come to see Felicia and Joan about the Merton story during the next week, but the school was abuzz with it.

"Did you ever hear anything so exciting?" one of the girls asked Joan. "She could be a millionaire heiress and not even know it."

Joan smiled.

"And just think," the other girl went on, "she's teaching school right here at Wellington. We all know her!"

At last, Friday came, and Felicia and Joan went to Miss Duncan to get permission to leave the campus for the weekend.

"I have only one question, Miss Bailey," the dean of women said.

"I think I know what that is," Joan said. "I have all my work up to date, as of this afternoon."

"That is as it should be," Miss Duncan told her. "And you are to have your work for Monday ready in time for classes. A weekend away from school is no excuse for being lax in your assignments."

An hour later, the three left Wellington and drove to Mountain View, New Hampshire.

"I thought perhaps the reporters would be out to see me," Miss Merton said, "and try to get another story, but they didn't come."

"I hope that means everyone has forgotten about it already," Joan put in. "I've been afraid the publicity would cause us a lot of trouble."

"If the people at Mountain View are only half as excited as the girls at school were," Felicia said, "the whole town will be at your old home when we drive in."

"I don't think it will affect the people at Mountain View that way," Miss Merton told her. "There may be some who will go out to the house to look around, but most of them will feel it is something that doesn't concern them."

They left the main highway and made their way up the valley to the little village.

"Do you think you'll find the box?" Joan asked.

Miss Merton shook her head.

"It doesn't seem likely after Mr. Gardell had the place gone over so carefully," she said, "but I won't be satisfied until we've looked for ourselves."

She was silent for a moment.

"I've been praying that we will get a clue to help me find out who I am."

"We've been praying too," Felicia answered.

They reached the little mountain community.

"Now where is it you live?" Joan asked.

"There's still a light in Mr. Gardell's office. Let's stop there first," Miss Merton said. I'll have to pick up the key."

As soon as the lawyer heard them in the reception room, he came out of his office.

"Cindy, I'm so glad you came!"

"I decided to take a look around the house myself," she answered.

"Great!" he replied. He lowered his voice. "I'd like to have you and your friends come into my office for a moment!"

As soon as the door closed behind them, the smile left his face.

"I suppose you saw that account in the papers," he began. "I'm terribly sorry about it. One of the men who was looking for the box chanced to overhear me talking about it. The next thing I knew, the reporter was asking all sorts of questions. I tried to get him to hold the story, but he refused."

"That's all right," Miss Merton answered. "I would have preferred no publicity, but I don't think it will cause any harm."

The lawyer's face clouded. "I'm not so sure," he said.

The tone in his voice startled Felicia. Joan noticed it too.

"What do you mean?" the teacher asked.

"The house has been broken into twice during the week."

"No!" Miss Merton cried.

"Now I don't think it's anything to get alarmed about," Mr. Gardell went on. "The chances are the intruder was just a curiosity seeker who was trying to find the box. Or it could have been a tramp who saw the place was empty and broke in without knowing anything about the box."

For a minute no one in the office spoke.

"You aren't planning on spending the night at the house, are you?" the lawyer asked.

Miss Merton shuddered.

"Not now. I wouldn't stay there for a thousand dollars."

"Neither would I," Joan put in.

"I don't think the guy will be back," Mr. Gardell told them. "We've got the night marshal keeping close watch on the house. In fact, he saw a man go in through a window night before last and almost caught him, so I'm sure the intruder is afraid to go back. But I still wouldn't want you girls there alone."

"You won't have to worry," Miss Merton said. "It's dark now. I think we'll wait until morning before we go out to the house."

"I think you're being very wise, Cindy," Mr. Gardell said. "There's no use taking any chances."

The girls and Miss Merton left the office and crossed the street to the cafe.

"What do you think now?" she asked softly.

"I don't know," Felicia answered, "but I get the chills every time I think about it."

"So do I," Joan confessed.

They entered the little cafe and went back to a small booth.

"I wonder why anyone would want to break into our house," the teacher said, "just to find that tin box. There's nothing in it that's valuable to anyone else."

"Maybe the thief wasn't even after the box," Joan said. "As Mr. Gardell said, it could have been someone who didn't even read that newspaper article."

"I suppose it could be at that," Miss Merton said without conviction, "but it seems like quite a coincidence. The house has been empty for months. Now, in the week since that story came out, someone has tried to break in twice."

"I have been thinking the same thing," Felicia put in. "Of course, it could be that whoever is trying to get the box doesn't realize there's nothing of real value in it."

"Or," Joan added, "someone is determined, for some good reason, to keep you from learning who your birth parents are."

Miss Merton's lips twitched nervously.

"That seems a cruel thing to do," she said somberly. "I can't believe anyone would want to do a thing like that."

"If Mr. Gardell is right in his guess that your parents were very wealthy," Joan continued, "there might be a very good reason for it. Anyone else who would inherit the money if you didn't show up would have a good reason for keeping you out of the picture."

For a minute no one spoke.

When the girls finished eating, they went to the hotel and registered. Felicia thought she would have difficulty sleeping, but she went to bed, and the next thing she knew, it was morning.

They were all up early and went directly to the place where Miss Merton and her parents used to live.

"There's the house," the teacher said, pulling to a stop before a neat two-story structure.

It had been painted white only a short time before. And, although it was quite old, everything was in good repair. Only the closed blinds and the weeds in the yard revealed that it was empty. There was a faded "For Sale" sign on the lawn near the sidewalk.

Miss Merton got out of the car quite deliberately and stood beside it.

"It makes me feel strange," she said, "to see the weeds in the yard and that 'For Sale' sign. Mom and Dad always kept up things."

The three of them walked slowly to the front door.

"I haven't been back here since the funeral," she said.

Joan shivered.

"I hope the character who broke in here hasn't been back," she said. "Or if he has, I hope he's gone by this time."

Felicia laughed uneasily.

"You can think of the most pleasant things," she said.

They stepped into the hallway.

The furniture was still where it had been before Mrs. Merton's death. The rugs were on the floor, and the curtains were on the windows. Only the dust and the odor of foul air indicated that no one lived there.

For several minutes Miss Merton walked from one room to the other. Neither Felicia nor Joan spoke.

"I'm not exactly sure where to start looking for the box," the teacher said at last. "Since the day I got a spanking for trying to open it, I don't recall having seen it."

There was a footstep on the front porch.

"M-M-Miss Merton!" Joan exclaimed. "What was that?"

They listened intently.

"T-T-There's someone out there," she repeated.

"You must be mistaken," Felicia countered. "I don't hear anything."

At that moment, there was a brisk rap on the door.

"Cindy!" a familiar voice called out. "Cindy Merton!"

"That's Wade Loring!" she exclaimed. "I wonder what he's doing here."

"Hi," he said, grinning broadly as she opened the door. "Surprised to see me?"

"Surprised?" Miss Merton echoed. "I'm not surprised at anything you do any more."

"Aren't you going to invite me in?"

"I didn't know you needed an invitation."

Felicia saw the look in Miss Merton's eyes. There was no doubt that she thought a great deal of Wade Loring.

"Would you mind telling me how you happened to trace us here?" Miss Merton asked.

"Not at all, my sweet." He flopped into a chair and draped his long legs over the arm. "I've got a spy who keeps me informed of every move you make."

"Now that is ridiculous," she said, and the color came to her cheeks. "Honestly, Wade, I don't know anyone quite like you."

"I'm glad of that," he answered. "But to give you a serious answer to your little question, you're something of a celebrity, Cindy. The minute I learned you were out of town, I said to myself, 'She's gone to Mountain View to chase down the great mystery.' So I hopped aboard my little, red chariot, and here I am."

"You may be sorry," she told him. "We'll put you to work."

"Madam," he informed her, "I am at your service. Your slightest wish is my command."

"Then I wish you'd get out of that chair," she said laughing, "and get busy."

"You do mean business, don't you?" he said, getting to his feet.

"Come on," Miss Merton said. "We've a lot of work to do if we're going over this house today."

They set to work systematically, going through the big house. Felicia and Joan took one room, and Miss Merton and her boyfriend another. They emptied cupboards and closets and poked about for loose boards or obscure corners where the box might have been hidden.

At noon they paused briefly for lunch.

"I'm willing to keep at this as long as you want to, Cindy," Wade Loring said. "But it looks like a losing proposition to me. Are you sure there ever was a tin box?"

"I'm positive," she countered. "That's one thing I'll never forget. I can still describe it perfectly."

"About all we have left is the attic and the basement," Wade said.

"And the garage and woodshed," Joan added. "And that little barn out back."

"I still say if a box were around here, we would have found it long before now," Wade said. "In fact, it should have been found before we even got here. You tell me the lawyer had men searching for two days, and the place was broken into twice. An object as large as a box wouldn't be that hard to find."

"I'm beginning to agree with you," Miss Merton answered, "but as long as we're here, we'd just as well finish the job."

They continued to work throughout the afternoon. The attic and basement were very dusty, and when darkness finally stopped the search, their clothes were grimy, and their faces were streaked with dirt.

"I'll say this," Wade Loring told them as they reluctantly left the house, "we all ought to get an A for effort."

"But we didn't find it," Miss Merton said dejectedly. "We didn't find a thing."

Wade looked down at her.

"Now tell me honestly," he said, "did you really expect to?"

"I suppose not," she answered truthfully, "but we were certainly praying and hoping."

They all went up to their rooms and began to clean up.

"I can't understand it," Joan said. "We didn't find a place that even looked as though it could have hidden a box like Miss Merton described."

"Frankly," Felicia answered, "it doesn't look as though we're going to find it."

"Wade Loring is a lot of fun, isn't he?" Joan asked, changing the subject.

Felicia nodded.

"He is a lot of fun," she agreed, "and it's easy to see why Miss Merton likes him. But that doesn't change the fact that he's not a Christian."

She took a deep breath.

"I hope Miss Merton realizes that before it's too late."

CHAPTER 7

DISAPPOINTMENT

Felicia and Joan waited for Miss Merton in the lobby of the hotel. She was fifteen minutes late and wore her coat and scarf.

"We thought we'd be eating here," Felicia said. "We'll have to get our wraps."

Miss Merton frowned.

"Wade asked me to have dinner with him," she explained. "I don't like to leave you girls, but he was so insistent. And after all, he did spend the day helping us."

"That's quite all right," Felicia answered. "Go ahead and have a good time. We'll manage very well."

"I'm sure you will."

"In fact," Joan added, "I'm so tired, I'd as soon eat and go right to bed."

Wade Loring came up just then.

"Sorry you girls can't go along," he said, smiling.

"I'll bet you are," Felicia answered good-naturedly.

"You are most understanding," he said as he and Miss Merton went out. "I shall instruct your teacher to give you an A."

"Talk especially hard for me," Joan called after him.

Wade guided Cynthia Merton to his car across the street.

"Those two are nice kids," he said. "I like them both."

"So do I," she answered. "They've been real friends. Almost the only friends I've made since I went to Wellington."

He opened the car door for her and went around on the other side.

"Where to?" he asked. "The Flame Room?"

"I'd rather not, Wade," she answered. "They serve a lot of liquor there."

He ruffled slightly.

"Just because we go there is no sign we'll be drinking," he retorted. "It so happens that I like their steaks."

"The Mountain Inn is just as nice," she suggested, "and it's only a few miles out of town."

"The Mountain Inn it is."

He jammed his foot on the accelerator, and the red sports car went bounding over the narrow, hard-surfaced road.

Cynthia caught her breath.

"You know, Cindy," Wade said at last, "I should be very angry with you."

She looked at him.

"Why?"

"You still haven't taken my ring back."

She glanced away and folded her hands in her lap.

"Did you hear me?" he asked.

"Yes," she said, "I heard you, Wade."

He drove on in silence.

"Are you going to take it back?" he asked.

She moistened her lips nervously. "I–I haven't decided yet," she said.

He slowed to a crawl and glanced at her.

"If you had a good reason, Cindy," he said, "just one good reason, I wouldn't say another word. If I thought you didn't love me, I wouldn't say anything more. I'm not about to throw myself at you or anyone else."

"I know that," she replied. "And I do love you, Wade. I suppose I'll always love you."

He lit a cigarette and inhaled deeply.

"Then why won't you marry me?" he insisted. "Answer me that."

"I–I've tried to explain," she said, stammering over the words. "You aren't a Christian. I–I'm afraid it wouldn't work out."

He snuffed out his cigarette angrily.

"Maybe I don't have this religion of yours," he said. "I'll admit I don't. But I don't think I'm so bad. I've got a good job, and I think I'm as honest as the next one."

She swallowed hard.

"And I'm not going to interfere with your going to church," he continued. "I'll give you my word."

"It isn't that," she said.

"Then what is it?" he demanded. "Don't you think I'm entitled to an answer?"

"I don't know whether I can find words to explain or not," she said, "but the Bible tells us we're not to marry those who aren't Christians. It says we're not to be unequally yoked together."

They reached the Mountain Inn. Wade pulled into the parking lot and stopped.

"I've already promised to quit drinking when we get married," he said. "I'll even go to church with you, if that'll make any difference."

She looked up at him, anguish in her eyes.

"Will you take back my ring, Cindy?" he whispered. "Will you?"

"I don't know," she said miserably. "I don't know."

* * *

Felicia and Joan were asleep when Miss Merton came back to the hotel. It was at breakfast the next morning that they saw her.

"Hi," Felicia said brightly, "did you have a nice time last night?"

"We had a lovely time," she said. "We drove out to the Mountain Inn. It's a beautiful place. I'll have to take you there the next time we come."

There was a short silence.

"You act very happy," Joan said at last. "You didn't happen to find the box, did you?"

Miss Merton shook her head. Her eyes were sparkling. "No," she replied, "but something happened that was better than that."

She broke into a smile and held out her hand to show them the diamond.

"I accepted Wade's ring again."

"I hope you'll be very happy," Felicia told her.

The smile left the teacher's face.

"Don't you like Wade, Felicia?" she asked.

"It isn't that," the girl answered. "Wade seems to be a very nice guy. But he isn't a Christian, is he?"

The young woman started, and for an instant, she looked away.

"He's promised to go to church with me," she answered. "As a matter of fact, he's going with us this morning."

Felicia and Joan went to Sunday school, but Miss Merton waited in the lobby for Wade Loring.

The four of them sat together through the church service.

"Well," Miss Merton said as she and Wade got into his car to drive back to the hotel, "what did you think of the service?"

He took out a cigarette and lit it.

"It was all right," he said.

"Is that all you've got to say?"

"I enjoyed it," he replied. "It was very interesting."

Her face revealed her disappointment.

"I'm sorry, Cindy," he said, "but I just can't go for that stuff. If it'll make you happy, I'll go to church with you, but I can't promise I'm going to believe what we hear there. I'm just not the religious kind."

Miss Merton was very quiet throughout dinner. They met Felicia and Joan again in the hotel lobby. "All set to go back to school?" Wade Loring asked.

"As ready as I'll ever be," Joan told him.

"It's too bad you didn't find that box," he continued, turning to Miss Merton. "I'm really very sorry. But I'm not surprised. I'm sure it's long gone. Maybe it was gone before your mother died."

"I'm disappointed too," she answered. "I thought surely we'd find something in the way of evidence."

"Did I ever tell you about the tin box I used to have?" he went on. "I used it to save pennies to buy a pony. I don't know what happened except that I didn't get the pony. Maybe my box disappeared too."

Miss Merton straightened suddenly.

"A pony!" she exclaimed. "That's it!"

They all stared at her.

"Whatever are you talking about?"

"Remember that little barn out back?" she went on. "Dad Merton built it for me when he got me a pony."

"What has that got to do with the tin box?" Felicia asked.

"My pony was so small she couldn't reach the bottom of the manger to get the hay out. So Dad put a board across about half way down. Under that board would make a perfect hiding place. And it's one place we haven't looked."

"It's about the only place we didn't look," Joan said.

Wade Loring shrugged his shoulders.

"I guess it won't hurt to go by there," he said. "It will only take a few minutes."

The girls got into the teacher's car, and Wade Loring followed them back to the Merton house.

"I have the strangest feeling," Miss Merton said breathlessly, "that the box is out there. I don't know why I didn't think of the manger before."

She pulled into the driveway and jumped out of the car. Felicia and Joan had to hurry to catch up with her.

"Wait for me!" Wade Loring called.

At the barn door, they paused, and he joined them.

"Now," he said, "we'll see if your precious tin box is here." He pushed past the girls and strode to the manger. "I'll–" he began. But his voice choked off.

"What's the matter?" Miss Merton demanded, moving toward him.

"Look," he said. "Someone has beaten us out here. The hay is out of the manger, and the board is loose."

Miss Merton caught her breath.

"The marks of the claw hammer are fresh too," Wade said. "It couldn't have been done more than a day or two ago."

Miss Merton turned away.

"I don't know why I didn't think of the manger yesterday," she said.

They started to leave, but Joan, who had brought along the flashlight, stepped up to the manger.

"We came this far," she said. "We'd just as well take a look."

"It's no use," Miss Merton said. "If it had been in there, it's gone now."

Nevertheless, Joan lifted the board and shined the light in the bottom of the manger.

"Do you see anything?" Felicia asked.

There was nothing in the manger, but she flicked the beam of light around the barn momentarily.

"What's that?" Felicia asked.

"I don't see anything."

"Over there under that old rug."

Joan moved the beam of light until it rested on a tattered rag rug someone had thrown in a corner. Felicia went over and lifted it.

"Oh!" she gasped, recoiling as though she had found a snake.

There, thrown carelessly under one corner of the rug, was a small tin box.

"That's it!" Miss Merton cried, her voice breaking with emotion. "That's it!"

She was trembling so, she could not pick it up.

Wade Loring did so with swift, sure movements.

For an instant he stood motionless. Then he looked up.

"It's empty, Cindy!" he said. "There's nothing in it!"

CHAPTER 8

ANOTHER CLUE

There was silence in the little barn. The only sound was that of labored breathing.

"That's the box," Miss Merton finally said. "I'd know it anywhere."

"Somebody beat us to it," Felicia managed.

"And," Wade Loring said, "whoever found it was so anxious, he couldn't wait to see what was in it. He broke the padlock right here."

Wade saw a glint of metal in the hay on the ground and stooped to pick up a tiny lock.

"This must be the lock your parents had on it, Cindy," he said.

"It is," she answered. "I remember it well."

"Maybe we can find something else around here," Joan said, sweeping the floor of the barn with the light.

"He surely would have taken everything in the box," Miss Merton said, "after going to all that trouble to get it."

Felicia turned back the rug and Joan began to cover the area with the flashlight. They were about to leave when the beam rested on a bright object almost buried in the hay.

"What's this?" Felicia murmured, stopping to dig it from the hay.

"A bracelet!" Joan cried. "A baby bracelet!"

Miss Merton and Wade Loring both crowded closer.

"Let me see!" the teacher said. Her voice was taut and thin.

She took the bracelet and began to turn it, examining it carefully.

"It's exquisite!" she said, more to herself than to her companions. "That ruby must be genuine. And it's mounted in white gold or platinum."

"It's an expensive piece of jewelry, all right," Wade Loring observed. "It didn't come from the dime store. That's for sure."

Miss Merton stepped outside to examine it in the sunlight.

"There are initials in it," she said, "J. N."

"Do you suppose it came out of that box?" Joan asked curiously.

"Where else?" Felicia retorted. "That's the only possible way it could have gotten out here in the barn."

She motioned Joan off to one side.

"Besides," she whispered, "I found something else just now."

Joan's eyes widened.

"What is it?" she asked. "Another bracelet?"

Felicia shook her head. With a glance at Wade Loring to be sure he wasn't watching, she opened her hand and showed Joan a yellowed bit of paper.

"What is it?"

"It may be an even more important clue than the bracelet," she whispered. "It's the postmark from a letter, and it's quite old."

"Aren't you going to show it to Miss Merton?" Joan asked.

"Not until we're on the way home," she said. "If she wants to tell Wade Loring about it, that's her business, but we can't do anything about chasing it down for at least another week. I don't want to tell a single soul about it."

After a time, Wade drove away, and the girls continued the trip back to Wellington. When they were out of town, Felicia showed Miss Merton the piece of paper she had found.

"I picked it up when I found the bracelet" she said, "but I didn't know whether you wanted Mr. Loring to know about it or not."

"It would have been all right," Miss Merton replied. She took it and examined it. "Hemely Park. I've never heard of a place by that name. Have you?"

The girls both shook their heads.

"And the name of the state is blurred so badly, we can't read it."

There was a short silence.

"Do you suppose it's important?" Miss Merton asked.

"It could be terribly important," Felicia said. "It might be from a letter your mother wrote to the Mertons after they took you to live with them."

The teacher nodded.

"But where is Hemely Park? That's the big question."

They drove on for some miles.

"There are only fifty states in the Union," Miss Merton said numbly. "And I suppose it could be located in any one of them."

"Maybe," Joan put in. "But the chances are, it is either in a state close by or in one your adoptive parents visited. They would have had some contact with the place."

"They were real stay-at-homes," the teacher answered. "I can only recall two vacations they ever took, and I don't think they left New Hampshire either time."

"Let's stop at the next gas station," Felicia suggested, "and get copies of some local maps they have, and we can search online."

They filled the car with gas, picked up the maps, and drove out to the edge of town where Miss Merton pulled off the highway and stopped at a roadside table.

They spread out the maps and began to go over them carefully.

It was Joan who located the town.

"Here it is!" she cried excitedly. "In the mountains of Vermont!"

"That's right," Miss Merton affirmed, as though she doubted it until she saw it herself. "And it's not so very far from either Mountain View or Wellington."

Joan burst into a broad smile.

"Isn't that luck to find it right off that way?" she asked. "I thought we'd have to hunt for hours."

"It may be lucky," Felicia said, "and it may not. There may be another Hemely Park, you know. It could even be in Canada."

"You would think of something like that," Joan said, "to spoil everything."

"There might be other towns by the name of Hemely Park," Miss Merton said. "That's true, but it isn't likely. I've never heard of a town by that name before." She studied the map once more. "Would you girls like to go up there with me during Thanksgiving vacation?"

"I–I don't know," Joan said uncertainly. "I haven't gotten my allowance yet, and I won't have it until December 1."

"I'll take care of the expenses," Miss Merton said. "But I don't want to go alone, and I don't know of anyone else I would feel free to ask."

"Miss Merton," Joan answered, "you've got yourself a companion."

"And how about you, Felicia?" the teacher asked.

"I wouldn't miss it for anything."

CHAPTER 9

BIRTH RECORDS

It seemed to Felicia and Joan that the days before Thanksgiving vacation would never pass. Fortunately, they had reports to make and homework to do that kept them busy.

Wade Loring was making regular trips to see Miss Merton, and she seemed happier and more contented than she had been since arriving at Wellington.

"She's certainly in love with him," Joan said. "Anybody can tell that much."

"And," Felicia added, "I think he's in love with her. He must be, or he wouldn't drive over here so often to see her."

"To tell you the truth, Felicia," Joan went on, "I can't blame her for going for him in a big way. He's really charming." She paused for a moment. "Maybe he'll decide to trust the Lord after they're married.

He did tell her he'd go to church with her regularly if it would make her happy."

"I don't think she can count much on that, do you?" Felicia asked. "I'm afraid she's only fooling herself when she thinks so."

Joan thought for a moment.

"I know you're right," she said, "but I feel so sorry for her. She loves him a great deal."

Felicia nodded.

"The mistake was made when she started going with him in the first place," she said. "If she had just been sure her dates were always Christians, she wouldn't be in a mess like this."

Wellington School for Girls dismissed at noon on the Tuesday before Thanksgiving Day to give students time enough to get home. Joan and Felicia were both ready to leave for Hemely Park after lunch, when the phone rang.

"It's Miss Merton," Felicia whispered to Joan, "and she sounds terrible."

"What's wrong?" Joan asked quickly. "Is she upset about something?"

"Nothing like that," Felicia answered. "She must have a cold or the flu or something. She's so hoarse she can hardly talk."

"There goes our trip to Hemely Park," Joan said, "and after we passed up a chance to go home."

When Felicia hung up the phone, Joan was unpacking.

"She can't go?" Joan asked. "That's just what I figured."

"She called the doctor a little while ago," Felicia said. "Miss Merton won't be able to get out of bed for several days."

Joan sighed.

"Just our luck!"

"Wait a minute, Joan!" Felicia exclaimed. "Don't unpack any more. Let's go over and see Miss Merton."

"What good will that do?" Joan asked.

"Maybe we can go to Hemely Park and look around," she said. "We might be able to get some information for Miss Merton, so she'll have some place to start looking when she gets an opportunity to go there."

At first, the teacher protested that they wouldn't want to go to the little mountain community alone.

"You'd better spend Thanksgiving with your parents," she said.

"It's too late for me," Joan answered. "They've already left to visit other relatives. If I don't go to Hemely Park, I'm stuck in the dorm alone."

"It would be great if you could go up there," Miss Merton said. "You might not learn very much, but if you got the names of some people I might contact, it could mean a great deal."

She insisted on giving them money enough to make the trip.

Felicia and Joan drove up to the little Vermont

community. It was dark when they got there. They checked in at the only motel and waited until morning to begin their search.

"Where do you think we ought to start?" Joan asked for the fifth time.

"We could find out who has lived here the longest," Felicia said, "and talk with them. They ought to remember if a baby was adopted from Hemely Park. That isn't done every day in a small town."

Joan took the bracelet from her handbag and looked at it once more.

"I'm glad Miss Merton let us bring this along," she said. "It might be an important clue."

"The initials J. N. could mean a lot," Felicia added, "if the bracelet actually belonged to Miss Merton when she was a baby."

"As Wade Loring said," Joan observed, "it is expensive. The stone is a genuine ruby."

Felicia's forehead crinkled thoughtfully.

"Ruby," she questioned, "ruby? Isn't that the birthstone for May?"

"I think so," Joan replied, "but I don't see what that has to do with it."

"If this belonged to Miss Merton," Felicia went on, her voice rising with excitement, "it could mean she was born in May. We could go to the courthouse, check the birth records, and see if any girl babies with the initials J. N. were born during the month of May twenty-five years ago."

"Felicia!" Joan exclaimed. "You're positively uncanny!"

The following morning, as soon as the courthouse opened, they hurried to the office where the birth records were kept.

A bald-headed, little man pushed back from the desk and came to them. His frown tightened as he fastened his gaze upon them.

"I'm Adrian Stokes," he announced with considerable pride. "Is there anything I can do for you?"

"We would like to look at the birth records for the month of May, twenty-five years ago," Felicia said.

He leaned on the counter, his eyes narrowing.

"And what do you want them for?" he asked suspiciously. "That was b'fore either of you was borned, unless I miss my guess."

"We–we were looking for a friend," Joan told him.

"What name are you lookin' for?" he persisted. "We don't have many births around here. Maybe I can tell you right off and save you a lot of time."

"We would like to look at the book, please," Joan said. "We want to learn the name of a baby girl with the initials J. N., who was born in May twenty-five years ago this spring."

Felicia thought Adrian Stokes stiffened slightly, as though he had touched his finger to a hot iron. His expression did not change.

"That's a right unusual request," he said, "but we get some strange ones now and then."

He went back to the safe. In a moment or two, he came out with a heavy book, deposited it on a table, and sat down before it.

"I don't recollect any baby girls born with those initials," he said, getting out his spectacles. "But we'll soon see."

He ran a stubby finger down the long column.

"There's nothing here," he said, looking up. "Didn't think there was."

"Are you sure?" Joan asked him.

His blue eyes flashed. "Young woman," he said, "if I wasn't sure, I'd have kept a-lookin' until I was. Now if you'll excuse me, I've got to get back to work."

He picked up the book and started back to the safe with it.

"And if I were you," he said, "I'd get on home and mind my own business. You aren't going to get anything done except bother people who are busy."

They thanked him and left.

"I've seen a lot of people who are friendlier than that," Joan said when they were out in the corridor. "You'd have thought we tried to rob a bank from the way he acted."

Felicia punched her in the ribs.

"S-s-shh," she warned.

"What's the matter?"

"He came out into the corridor and is watching us."

Joan gasped, took Felicia by the arm, and hurried her down the stairs.

CHAPTER 10

NEWSPAPERS!

The girls left the courthouse and walked across the street.

"I didn't like that man," Joan said. "He gave me the goose bumps the way he looked at us."

"Me, too," Felicia said.

"You know," Joan continued, "we don't even know that there isn't a birth of a girl baby with the initials J. N. registered in May twenty-five years ago. Old Beady Eyes looked in the book. We didn't get a squint at it."

"That's right. We could probably get the information from the State Capitol. They would have it."

"But they wouldn't be able to find it unless we had more information than we have now," Joan said. "I don't think they'd even start a search if we only knew the initials and the month and year of birth."

"I suppose not," Felicia said. "But what are we going to do?"

Joan shook her head.

"You know," Felicia went on, "when we were back in Wellington, it seemed it would be so easy once we got here."

They went to the car and sat down.

"I suppose we could find some of the old-timers around here. Maybe they could give us some information."

Joan drew in her breath sharply.

"I've just thought of something," she said. "Someone is trying hard to keep Miss Merton from finding out who she is. If that's true, whoever it is lives here or is around here right now trying to stop her if she comes to town."

Felicia's face blanched.

"That means we've got to be very careful with whom we talk," she said, "or we could get into real trouble. Maybe we'd better drive around a while and think things out."

Joan backed away from the curb and went down the narrow, mountain road. The wind was coming up, and it looked like more snow.

"I don't know why we didn't think of it before," Felicia said with a suddenness that startled her companion.

"Why didn't we think of what?" Joan asked.

"Of going to the newspaper office. They keep files of all the old papers. And a small-town paper always reports births."

"Now," Joan said excitedly, "you have moved the stew to the front burner."

She turned around at the nearest crossroads, drove back to town, and stopped in front of the newspaper office.

"The old papers are filed over there," the editor said with a wave of his hand. "But I don't think you'll find much of anything in our old papers. We have had a daily for years, but mostly we're a family newspaper. We don't print much real exciting news."

"I think perhaps we can find what we want," Joan told him. "Thank you."

They went back to the old files and started through them. They were all there, a copy of each paper stacked according to week and month and year.

"Let's see now," Felicia said, blowing the dust off a stack so she could see the date on the top paper. "Here are the papers of twenty years ago."

Joan found another stack and checked them.

"Here we go," she said, keeping her voice low.

They soon found copies of the paper for the month of May.

"You take part of them," Felicia said, "and I'll take the rest. It shouldn't take too long."

"We want to be sure we don't miss it," Joan cautioned. "Sometimes items like that are in small type."

They looked over each paper carefully, reading all the birth notices.

"Not a thing," Joan said at last. "We've gone through all of them."

Felicia ran her finger over the top paper on the January stack.

"That's strange," she said.

Joan looked at her questioningly.

"Did you blow the dust off these papers before you started looking at them?" Felicia asked.

Joan shook her head.

"There wasn't any dust on them."

"But there was dust on all the rest," Felicia went on.

Joan leaned forward. "Do you mean you think someone came over here ahead of us," she asked, "and went through these papers?"

"Exactly."

Felicia checked the papers for May by date.

"And," she said, "the paper for May 19 is missing!"

"Somebody must have taken it out," Joan whispered. "Newspapers always keep a complete file of their old papers."

The girls stared at one another.

"We are onto something!" Joan said. "I knew it! When we saw that funny look in Adrian Stokes's eyes, I knew it!"

"Let's get out of here," Felicia murmured, "where we can talk."

"We could ask the editor if someone came in a little while ago and asked to look at the papers," Joan went on.

But Felicia was against it.

"We'd better not let him know we suspect any-thing strange is going on," she said.

The owner of the paper turned as he walked by.

"Well," he said, smiling pleasantly, "did you find what you were looking for?"

"Not yet, thank you," Felicia answered.

"Didn't think you would," he said. "As I told you, we never print much of anything important."

They thanked him and left the office.

On the street, the girls turned to face one another.

"Now what do we do?" Joan asked. "We've been stumped every way we've turned."

"There's got to be some way we can get the informa-tion we want," Felicia said. "Without telling everyone we meet what we're after and why."

"But how?" Joan asked. "Answer me that!"

"Do you recall that the paper always gave the name of the officiating doctor when a birth was reported?" Felicia asked.

"What good is that going to do?"

"If the doctor is still around here, we might be able to persuade him to go through his records and see if he took care of the mystery baby when she was born."

Joan saw that people were staring at them.

"Come on," she said. "Let's go have a dish of ice cream. Then we can talk without looking so suspicious."

They went into the shop and sat down. Almost

immediately, Felicia took out a pencil and began to write on the corner of a paper napkin.

"Now what are you doing?" Joan asked.

"Writing down the names before I forget them. Did you notice the names of any other doctors than Dr. Harold Roberts and Dr. Cleve N. Newmeyer?"

Joan shook her head.

"To be perfectly honest with you, Felicia," she said, "I didn't even notice those. I was looking for the names of babies, not doctors."

"It's worth a try anyway," Felicia said.

While the waitress was bringing their ice cream, she talked with the owner of the shop. He was an older man with gray hair and a pleasant smile.

"I remember old Doc Newmeyer, all right," he said. "I guess everybody in Hemely Park remembers him."

"What about Dr. Roberts?" Felicia asked. "Dr. Harold Roberts?"

"I can't say that I remember much more about him than his name. He was just a young guy. Came here and tried to open a practice, but it didn't go over. Everybody liked old Doc too well. I don't think he was here more than a year at the most."

"I suppose Dr. Newmeyer took care of most of the births around here," Felicia ventured.

"I'll say he did." He chuckled to himself. "Old Doc was always careless about things like reporting births and so on. Hardly a month goes by that someone doesn't wander in here hoping to get a look at Doc's records, so they'll have the proof they need for a birth certificate."

"Thank you," Felicia said. "Thank you very much."

She started back to the booth but stopped and returned to the counter.

"I don't like to bother you again," she asked, "but can you tell me where we might find Dr. Newmeyer's records?"

He looked at her curiously.

"We are seeking information for a friend," she said.

"I figured you were too young to have been one of Doc's babies," he said. He scratched his head. "Hanscomb Clarke has the keys, I reckon," he answered. "He's the lawyer handling old Doc's estate."

They finished their ice cream and went directly to the lawyer's office.

"There are a lot of records out at old Doc Newmeyer's house," he said. "He had his office there, and he has them in some big files. I've never had time to go through them."

"Would it be possible for us to go out there?" Felicia asked. "We are looking for some important information for a friend of ours."

The lawyer eyed them for a moment.

"I don't have time to go out there myself," he said. "If you'll come back the first of the week, my secretary will be back. I'll have her go with you."

"But we can't do that," Joan blurted. "We have to be back in school Sunday night."

"I'm sorry. I'm afraid I can't help you then," Mr. Clarke answered.

The girls stared at one another. Then Felicia remembered Mr. Gardell.

"Do you know Mr. Henry Gardell of Mountain View, New Hampshire?" she asked.

He smiled slightly.

"Do you know Henry?" he asked. "We've been at Bar Association Conventions together."

"Would you please call and ask him if we're all right?" Felicia asked.

He looked up a number and made the call.

"You talk to him," he said, handing the phone to Felicia. "I'll listen on the extension."

After the conversation was finished, the attorney was smiling.

"I'm sorry to have caused you so much trouble," he said, taking a key from the desk drawer, "but you see my position. I must be careful with the property entrusted to me."

"Thank you very much," Felicia said. "We'll return the key as soon as we've finished with it."

"That's quite all right," he said.

They left his office and drove to the old Newmeyer house on the edge of town. It was a huge, gaunt, old building, its porches ornate with scroll work and pillars and fancy railings that had one day made it a show place, but now caused it to look old and dowdy.

It had been almost closing time when they got

the call through to Mr. Gardell and left Mr. Clarke's office. So it was nearly dark when Joan pulled up before the Newmeyer house.

"I don't know if I want to go in there or not," she said. "Br-r-r-r! That gives me the shakes."

"We aren't going to find out anything sitting here," Felicia said.

"There won't be any electricity on," Joan reminded her, "and that's an awfully big house. Especially in the dark."

"But we're not going to be in it very long," Felicia said, scoffing. She opened the glove compartment and took out the flashlight. "After all," she continued, "we're not breaking into the place. We've got the key and permission to enter."

"That, Felicia Cartright," Joan began, "is not what I'm worried about."

The two girls made their way up to the front door of the house. They opened it and went into the living room.

"Turn on that flashlight," Joan said, her voice taut. "I–I want to see if th-th-there's anyone in here b-b-before we go any farther."

Felicia switched on the light and shined it across the large living room.

"Joan!" she scolded. "Don't be like that! You'll have me scared too!"

"You can't kid me. You're scared already."

They made their way to the living room and finally into Dr. Newmeyer's office.

"Let's get into these files," Joan said. "I want to find what we came for and get out of here."

There were half a dozen huge files in the office, and it took them a few minutes to locate the dusty, black journals containing the records of the doctor's calls and patients, year by year.

"Nobody's been in here before us," Joan observed, wiping the dust off the books. "That's for sure."

Felicia began to check through the big journals year by year. At last, she found the one she was seeking.

"This is the one," she said.

At that very instant, there was a sound outside the house.

"Felicia!" Joan cried in a hushed voice. "Turn off that light! There's somebody out there! Just outside the front porch!"

CHAPTER 11

A WARNING

For a tense, breathless minute, Felicia and Joan crouched there, listening. Their breathing was labored, and their hands were moist with perspiration.

"Did you hear it?" Joan asked.

Felicia shook her head. "I didn't hear a thing," she said.

"I did." Joan's voice was quavering. "There's someone out there, I tell you!"

"We can't stay here," Felicia whispered. "If there's someone out there, he'll be in here in a minute!"

They huddled together, not daring to move.

"Maybe he's gone," Joan whispered at last.

They heard the noise again. This time it was louder.

"There it is!" Joan exclaimed. "I–"

Felicia laughed nervously. "Do you know what that is?" she asked. "It's nothing but a hoot owl."

The silence was electric.

"A hoot owl?" Joan repeated skeptically.

"A hoot owl," Felicia assured her.

"Well," Joan said, "you can't say I'm not alert."

Felicia got to her feet and picked up the journal once more.

"Let's get out of here," she managed. "We can take this to the motel and bring it back in the morning."

"Sounds like the best idea you've had since we got here," Joan replied.

They left the house hurriedly and drove back to the motel. As they turned in, they saw a familiar car parked in the lot.

"Look!" Felicia exclaimed. "There's Miss Merton's car."

The teacher must have been watching for them. As they got out of the car, she joined them.

"Good evening, girls," she said.

"We thought you were sick," Felicia countered, her voice tinged with surprise.

"I felt better soon after you left," Miss Merton said, "so I persuaded the doctor to let me join you here for Thanksgiving."

They went into the motel together.

"Are we ever glad to see you!" Joan exclaimed. "And have we got things to tell you!"

They related all that had happened since they arrived at Hemely Park the evening before.

"And now," Felicia said, "we've got the journal

that belonged to the busiest doctor in Hemely Park. We were going to look at it when we got back here."

Miss Merton locked the door. They spread the book out on the floor and got down on their knees in front of it.

"Look at this notation," Felecia said, reading aloud, "'May 2, saw 26 patients. 3 of them sick.' I can see now what the man meant when he said the doctor had such sketchy records."

"Maybe he didn't list all the births," Joan said. "Wouldn't that be a revolting development?"

"I'm sure he'll have them listed in some way," Miss Merton said without looking up. "We used to have an old doctor like that in Mountain View. He was careless about his accounts and everything, but he had an accurate record of the babies he helped into the world. He was very proud of that."

They continued through the book, day by day, struggling to read the cramped, hurried writing.

"We might find it and not be able to read it," Joan muttered.

They came across births, one or two a week, but no baby girl with the initials J. N.

"Let's go through that again," Miss Merton said. "We could have missed it."

They started with May and thumbed through the journal a second time, going over it slowly, line by line.

"Wait a minute!" Felicia exclaimed, pointing over Joan's shoulder. "What's this?"

"No initials there," Joan said.

"That's just it."

Miss Merton read the notation aloud. "'May 18, 11:35 p.m. Baby girl 6 lbs. 3 ½ ounces. No charge. Miss Donna Clay, assisting nurse.'"

"That's strange," she said. "No initials or name or anything."

"But look how careless he was when it came to keeping records," Felicia put in. "He could have been tired when he noted it and forgotten to put down the name. If the baby were born to a poor family who couldn't pay, he wouldn't have needed more of a record than this."

"I suppose you're right," Miss Merton said, "but it does seem strange."

"The name of the nurse who assisted him is here," Joan said. "If we could find her, she might give us the information we need."

Miss Merton read the doctor's journal account a third time.

"It sounds like a wild goose chase," she said. "We could go to a great deal of trouble and find that the baby could have been named most anything. But it's the only real clue we've got."

"We haven't had dinner yet," Felicia said. "Why don't we see if the motel owner remembers Miss Donna Clay. And if she's still around here, we can look her up after we eat."

"Good idea!" Miss Merton said. "Why don't you see him while I wash up?"

"I suppose she could have married," Felicia explained to the motel proprietor. "But about twenty-five years ago she was single, and her name was Clay. She was a nurse who helped Dr. Newmeyer."

He thought for a time.

"I can't recollect any girl by the name of Clay," he said, "but let me talk to my wife."

When he came back, he was smiling.

"Sure," he said, "I know who it is now. She's Mrs. Scott Glenser. Lives in a little, white house just west of town. It was that name Clay that threw me. Old Doc brought her here from Boston. None of her kin ever lived here."

They went to a café for dinner and drove out to the Glenser house. Mrs. Glenser came to the door; a tall woman with a hard face and eyes that were cold and unfriendly.

"Yes," she said, her words clipped and expressionless, "I used to be Dr. Newmeyer's nurse, but I remember very little about the cases we had. That was a long while ago. A very long while ago."

"We were wondering about one entry in his books," Miss Merton said. "It was the birth of a baby girl twenty-five years ago last May."

"I'm sorry," the woman answered, "but I can be of no help to you at all. There is no need in your wasting your time or mine."

With that she slammed the door, leaving them standing in the darkness.

"Now what do you make of that?" Felicia asked.

The teacher sighed wearily and wiped her hand across her face.

"I don't know," she said dejectedly. "I'm so tired and discouraged and confused that I almost feel like giving up and going back to Wellington."

"We can't do that yet," Joan said. "Someone here in Hemely Park knows something. We've got to keep on until we find out who it is and what he knows."

Miss Merton shook her head.

"I wish I shared your enthusiasm, Joan," she said, "but I'm almost ready to give up."

Joan drove them back to the motel and locked her car for the night.

They went into the room Felicia and Joan shared.

"I'm sure Mrs. 'Whatever-her-name-is' knew a lot more than she would tell us," Joan said.

"There was no standing there arguing with Mrs. Glenser," Felicia replied, "that's for sure. She spoke her little piece and slammed the door."

"Frankly," Miss Merton said, "I don't know which way to turn. Every lead we get ends up in a blind alley."

They were still talking when there was a sharp knock at the door.

"Now who could that be?" Miss Merton asked.

"Maybe it's the man who owns the motel," Joan said laughing, "asking us not to make so much noise."

"If we make any less," Felicia put in, "I think we'd all fall asleep."

She spoke as she went to the door.

There was a second knock. And as Felicia turned the doorknob, heavy footsteps were heard along the walk toward the back of the motel.

"That's strange," Felicia said, looking out.

"What is it?" Miss Merton asked, coming up beside her.

"Whoever was here turned and ran as I opened the door."

"If that's somebody's idea of a joke," Joan said, "I–" She stopped and looked down. "What's this?"

She picked up an envelope that had been dropped inside the storm door.

"What is it?" Miss Merton asked.

Joan's face went pale as she stared at it, and her hands began to tremble.

"LEAVE HEMELY PARK TONIGHT!
LAST WARNING!"

CHAPTER 12

THE MYSTERY SOLVED

Felicia, Joan, and Miss Merton stared at the crude, grease-smudged note. It had been made by clipping letters from the headlines of newspapers.

"Why would anyone send us this?" Felicia asked, reading the note again. "We haven't found out a single thing."

"No," Joan answered. "We haven't found out anything definite yet. But don't you think we're closer to finding out something than we realize?"

"You must be right," Miss Merton observed. "The person who wrote this note thinks we're getting close to unraveling the mystery, or he would never have risked sending it."

Joan took the note and began to examine it.

"What are you doing, Joan?" Felicia asked her. "Looking for fingerprints?"

"The only fingerprints would be our own," she

answered. "We've all pawed it so much we couldn't get a decent fingerprint even if we had the equipment."

"What are you doing?" Miss Merton asked.

"I'm trying to get one of these letters off," the girl said.

"Don't do that!" the teacher protested. "The police will want it intact."

"Do you recognize any of these letters, Felicia?" Joan asked.

"I'm not sure. Should I recognize them?"

"Look at that Y, then the T in 'tonight,'" Joan continued.

"They don't look different than any of the others," her companion said. "I think they all must have been taken from the same paper. At least the type is all the same."

"I'm not talking about the type," Joan said. By this time, she was getting excited. "Look at the paper! It's old and yellow!"

"That's right!" Felicia exclaimed. "It looks very much like the old papers we went through in the newspaper office." She put the note up to her nose and sniffed. "And it smells like them too. Musty."

"Whatever are you two talking about?" Miss Merton broke in. "What difference does it make if those two letters were cut from an old paper. A lot of people have old papers."

"It just might make a great deal of difference," Felicia said.

She took the paper and bent it carefully. The glue cracked.

"Now," she said, "I'm getting the T."

She removed the Y and turned the letters over.

"Look at that date!" Joan cried. "It's from the paper that was taken from the newspaper files!"

It was very plain, in spite of the glue.

"May 19."

Felicia turned to the big, black journal.

"I want to show you something," she said, her hands shaking. "Look at the date this notation was made in the journal. It's May 18."

"Is that significant?" Miss Merton asked, a question in her voice.

"If a child is born on the night of May 18," Felicia said, "the birth would have been reported in the paper on May 19, wouldn't it?"

"I guess so," the teacher said.

"I'm convinced that's what happened here," Felicia went on. "This birth record is the one the guy who stole the newspaper from the files wanted to keep from us."

"That would mean it's *my* birth!" Miss Merton exclaimed.

Joan opened her purse and took out the little bracelet.

"There's something else that just occurred to me," she said. "It's so obvious none of us even thought of it."

"What's that?" Felicia asked.

"The initials in this bracelet are J. N.," she said, "and Dr. Newmeyer's name starts with N."

"That's right!" Felicia exclaimed.

"If the birth that's recorded here is one in the Newmeyer family," Joan went on, "that could account for the fact that the doctor didn't put the name in the book. It wasn't necessary because that was one he would never forget."

Miss Merton's eyes were wide and staring.

"And," Felicia put in, "that would also account for the fact that there was no charge for the doctor's services."

"To fill in the rest of the picture," Joan concluded, looking at Miss Merton, "Dr. Newmeyer's estate is being settled right now. Whoever is going to inherit his money could be afraid we are going to find the evidence that will prove you are his granddaughter."

The teacher got to her feet and paced the floor.

"I don't know what to think," she said. "It scares me somehow. I don't know whether I want to find out more or go back to Wellington."

"You can't quit now, Miss Merton," Felicia told her firmly. "You've got to find out for sure whether or not you are Dr. Newmeyer's granddaughter."

"But there is this note to think about," Miss Merton said. "We have no way of knowing how far the person who sent it will go to keep us from finding out the truth. I can't let you girls keep on when it may put you in real danger."

Silence gripped them.

"I don't believe the note writer wants to harm us," Felicia said. "He just wants to scare us out of Hemely Park."

"We hope," Joan added under her breath.

"And," Felicia said suddenly, "I think the proof we've got to have is at the Newmeyer house. If you actually are a member of that family, there ought to be something out there to prove it."

"If whoever left us this note doesn't get out there and destroy it before we can find it," Joan said. "He found the tin box, you know."

"That is exactly what I was thinking," Felicia went on. "Our only chance is to get there first."

"You aren't serious about that, are you?" Miss Merton demanded.

"As serious as I've ever been. We can get our suitcases and hurry out of the motel as though we're scared. We can drive through town on the highway, circle, and come back to the Newmeyer house."

Joan swallowed hard.

"Tonight?" she echoed.

"Tonight."

"I believe you're right at that," Miss Merton said, coming to a sudden decision. "Our friend who left the note will probably hang around for a while to see if his threat worked. If we drive away, he'll think we're scared out and the coast is clear."

"And," Felicia added, "we'll have time to get back to the Newmeyer house."

"I've got one question," Joan put in. "What if our playmate comes out while we're there to destroy the evidence we're looking for?"

Felicia blinked.

"That," she said, "is a chance we'll have to take."

They packed their suitcases hurriedly, threw them into the cars, and drove away. Joan and Felicia followed Miss Merton down the narrow, main street toward the highway that led to Wellington.

"I don't know whether I like this or not," Joan said uneasily. "If we were smart, I think we'd head this car for Wellington and not stop until we get there."

"Listen to you," Felicia said. "You know you wouldn't miss this any more than Miss Merton and I would."

"That's what has me worried," Joan continued. "I've been around you so much, I'm getting just like you. And it's not safe."

Miss Merton drove down the highway a mile or so and turned off on a narrow, winding side road. Once out of sight of the highway, she stopped.

"You girls had better lock your car and leave it here," she said, "and ride the rest of the way with me."

"If something's going to happen," Joan said, "I suppose it's better to have it happen to all three of us."

Miss Merton laughed.

"My, you're cheerful and optimistic tonight!"

"I've been with Felicia before," Joan countered. "I know what it's like to help her in one of her brainstorms."

Miss Merton slowed her car.

"Perhaps we had better go back," she said quietly. "We certainly don't want to take any chances. We probably wouldn't find anything in that old house anyway."

"Oh, no!" Joan exclaimed. "Don't pay any attention to me. I wouldn't miss this for anything, I–I think."

"She just has to give us a certain amount of static," Felicia explained. "When we stop at the Newmeyer house, she'll probably be the first one out of the car."

"And the first to turn and run if we see anyone," Joan added.

They drove to the Newmeyer place and turned in the narrow, weed-grown lane.

"I think we'll park back here behind this clump of trees," Miss Merton said. "Then if anyone goes by, we won't be seen from the road."

The girls got out of the car and went up to the front door of the house. Earlier in the evening the moon had been out, but now clouds covered it. The rising wind rattled shutters and sighed eerily through the trees.

"Got that flashlight handy, Felicia?" Joan whispered.

"It's right here, but I don't think I ought to turn it on until we get inside."

Joan inserted the key in the lock, and the door swung open with a protesting creak.

Miss Merton shivered.

"I don't know whether I dare take another step or not," she said in a weak voice.

Nevertheless, they went into the house and down the hall to the room Dr. Newmeyer used for an office.

"I suppose we'd better start in here," the teacher said. "We can go to the other rooms if we don't find anything."

"What are we looking for?" Joan asked.

"I don't know for sure," Miss Merton said. "A family Bible, old letters, a diary. Maybe even some legal papers. Anything like that could contain the evidence we're looking for."

"Now where do you suppose he would keep things like that?" she mused.

"In the files," Joan suggested.

"I'm not sure," Felicia countered. "He wouldn't want to get his personal things mixed with the records of his office."

"I believe you're right at that," Miss Merton said. "Is there a library in the house?"

Felicia shook her head.

"There's no library, but there is a shelf of books along one side of the living room."

Miss Merton took the light.

"Let's go in there first," she said. "That's the logical place."

They moved silently through the creaking, old house to the big living room.

"I don't know whether we'll ever get out of here or not," Joan whispered. "Just listen to this place. It sounds like a ghosts' convention."

Felicia laughed.

"How many ghosts' conventions have you attended?" she asked.

"Two, counting this one and the next. And believe me, they aren't much fun."

The beam of light sought out the bookshelves along the wall.

"Now," Miss Merton said, "let's look for a family Bible, a diary, or something personal like that."

It was Joan who found the album.

"Here's something," she managed in a hoarse whisper.

"Let's see it," Felicia said. "What is it?"

"A family picture album," she continued.

She opened it, but Miss Merton moved the light away.

"There's got to be a family Bible here somewhere," she said. "Everyone has a family Bible."

"What will we do with these things after we find them?" Joan asked. We can't take personal things out of here, can we?"

"I don't think Mr. Clarke would care if we took them and brought them back in the morning," Felicia said.

"Now you're talking sense," Joan answered. "The sooner we get out of here the–the better it'll be."

"Here's a Bible," Miss Merton put in. "I–"

She stopped, listening intently.

"Did you hear anything?" she asked.

"It was probably just the wind," Joan answered.

"It didn't sound like the wind to me," the teacher went on, moving toward the window. "Turn out the light, Felicia."

Joan gasped at the sudden darkness.

"This is almost as bad as being seen," she quavered.

"There's someone coming up the lane with his lights out," Miss Merton whispered.

"I knew it!" Joan exclaimed. "I knew we'd get caught out here!"

"We aren't caught yet," Miss Merton announced with firm determination. "Come on. We've got to get out of here before that guy has time to get in."

They started toward the front door, but before they could reach it, they heard a footstep on the porch.

"Quick!" the teacher ordered. "In here!"

She pushed them into a little closet and almost closed the door.

They clung to one another, hardly daring to breathe.

A minute passed, and they heard a window in the living room being forced open.

"Hurry up, Adrian," a masculine voice said. "We've got a lot to do before those girls get back here."

"Don't you worry about those girls, Glenser," a

familiar voice answered. "When they got that note, they shucked out of town so fast they probably left half of their stuff at the motel."

"Adrian Stokes and Scott Glenser, the husband of Dr. Newmeyer's nurse," Felicia thought. "Now what are they doing here? And why?"

"I don't know why that girl had to get wind of this just before old Newmeyer's estate was settled," Glenser grumbled. "Another two months and it would all have been over. The time limit would have run out, and Clarke could have turned the money over to Donna and me."

"I tell you there isn't a thing to worry about," Stokes said. "I went to Mountain View and found that little tin box the papers were screaming about. I wouldn't let those two kids look at the books in the courthouse, and as soon as they left, I went over to the newspaper office and destroyed the paper that carried the account of the birth. And by the way, that's something that's going to cost you plenty."

"I told you I'd cut you in, didn't I?" Glenser continued. "Come on, let's take what we came after and get out of here. I don't like this. I don't like it at all."

They walked quietly past the closet where the girls were hiding and on into the office.

As soon as they were gone, Joan turned to Miss Merton. "Let's get out of here! They'll catch us for sure."

"We can't go out the front door," the teacher said. "It squeaks."

"How about the window?" Felicia suggested. "I think they left it open."

They tiptoed out of the closet, down the hall, and into the living room.

"I hope we don't stumble over something," Joan whispered.

Their eyes were so accustomed to the darkness of the house that they could see the open window clearly. They made their way to it and climbed out.

"Now what do we do?" Felicia whispered.

"Get out to the car," Joan said. "Push it far enough from the house so they won't hear us start it and get out of here just as fast as we can."

They ran across the lawn to the clump of trees where the car was hidden and pushed it down the lane.

"Now," Felicia said, sighing her relief, "we can relax a little."

"Not until we get out of town," Joan countered. "When those guys find that the information they are looking for is gone, they'll start looking for us. And I, for one, wouldn't want to be around if they caught us."

"Neither would I," Miss Merton said, breathing heavily. "I think we'd better go to one of the neighboring towns to spend the night and come back here tomorrow."

"We can get in touch with Mr. Clarke," Felicia suggested. "He was very nice. He'll help us."

They made their way to the place where they had left Joan's car and drove to the neighboring town fourteen miles away.

"Now," Joan said, stopping before the town's only hotel, "we're safe. I didn't know whether we were going to make it or not."

They registered and went up to their rooms.

"Aren't we going through this stuff?" Joan asked.

"We're so tired, I don't think we could find it," Miss Merton said. "Besides, we know the truth now. It's just a matter of finding the entries that will prove it. I am sure we will all be able to do a much better job in the morning."

They went to bed, and the next thing they knew, the sun was streaming in the window. Joan rolled over and glanced at the clock.

"Felicia!" she exclaimed. "Look what time it is! It's after nine!"

The girl sat straight up in bed. "And I thought I wouldn't sleep at all."

They dressed hurriedly.

"I'll go in and see Miss Merton," Joan said. "Why don't you call Mr. Clarke and talk with him?"

When Joan entered the adjoining room, Miss Merton was sitting on the bed, the Bible and album on her lap.

"Have you found anything?" Joan asked.

Miss Merton looked up.

"A great deal," she said. Joan thought she saw tears in her eyes. "There's no doubt about it now. I am Dr. Newmeyer's granddaughter."

"I knew it!" Joan exclaimed. "I just knew it!" Then Felicia came bursting into the room.

"I just talked with Mr. Clarke!" she said excitedly. "He told me why Mr. Glenser is so concerned. Dr. Newmeyer only had one child – your father, Miss Merton. After he died and you were adopted out, the doctor made a new will. If the lawyer was unable to find you five years after his death, the entire estate was to go to Mrs. Glenser, who had been his nurse."

"That explains some things," Joan said. "Why Mrs. Glenser was so unfriendly, for example."

"And," Felicia went on, "Adrian Stokes is Mrs. Glenser's brother, which accounts for his actions."

"There's one question it doesn't answer," Joan said. "If Dr. Newmeyer thought so much of you, why would he let someone else adopt you after his son died? And why didn't your mother keep you?"

"I think I have the answer in the family album," Miss Merton said. "Here on this page, where my hand and footprints were put, is a letter."

She took it out and read it to them.

"'Dear Dad Newmeyer,'" she began. "It's from my mother," she explained, her voice shaky.

"I am so sorry to have to write you this, but I have been in a sanitarium with a nervous breakdown for more than a year. I was so ill, I didn't know or care what happened.

"'Today I learned that Fred let someone take little Jane, and I don't know who has her or where she is. I'm so heartbroken I don't know what to do.

"'You were right about Fred. He always promised he would go to church and change after we were married. You warned me against going with someone who wasn't a Christian after the first date I had with him, but I thought it was just that you didn't want me to marry again.

"'Now that it's too late, I see what you meant. Please forgive me. If I had listened to you, we would still have our little girl, and I would be happy and well. . . .'"

Miss Merton started to cry softly.

"And," she continued, "there was a newspaper clipping in the envelope dated the same day as the letter. Mother went out to mail the letter and, on the way back, she stepped in front of a truck and was killed instantly."

Miss Merton's voice choked.

"How terrible!" Felicia exclaimed.

There was a long silence.

"I learned two things this Thanksgiving morning,"

the teacher said at last. "I found out who I am, and I found out something else."

The girls listened quietly.

"Somehow I had the idea that marrying Wade Loring was my last chance for marriage," she said, her voice trembling. "Now I see that it is much better to be single than to be married to a man who doesn't know Jesus as his personal Savior."

With great deliberation, she removed her ring and put it into her purse.

THE
FELICIA CARTRIGHT
SERIES

Felicia Cartright, a petite blonde who is one of the most popular students at Wellington School for Girls, has a surprising inclination toward mysteries. If a mysterious situation arises, it either makes its way to Felicia, or Felicia somehow finds it. Though this is a bit trying for her happy-go-lucky roommate, Joan Bailey, it does prevent life from becoming monotonous. It also enables Bernard Palmer, the popular author of the "Danny Orlis" books, to write an entertaining series of stories for girls aged twelve to eighteen.

The mysteries range from a valuable missing antique to an attempt by claim jumpers to steal a deposit of tungsten ore. There's excitement and action galore—but there's also spiritual guidance and blessing because Felicia and her partner-in-adventure love the Lord and take Him into account in all their experiences.

AVAILABLE FROM WWW.ANEKOPRESS.COM